ANIMAL BATTLE

I0877070

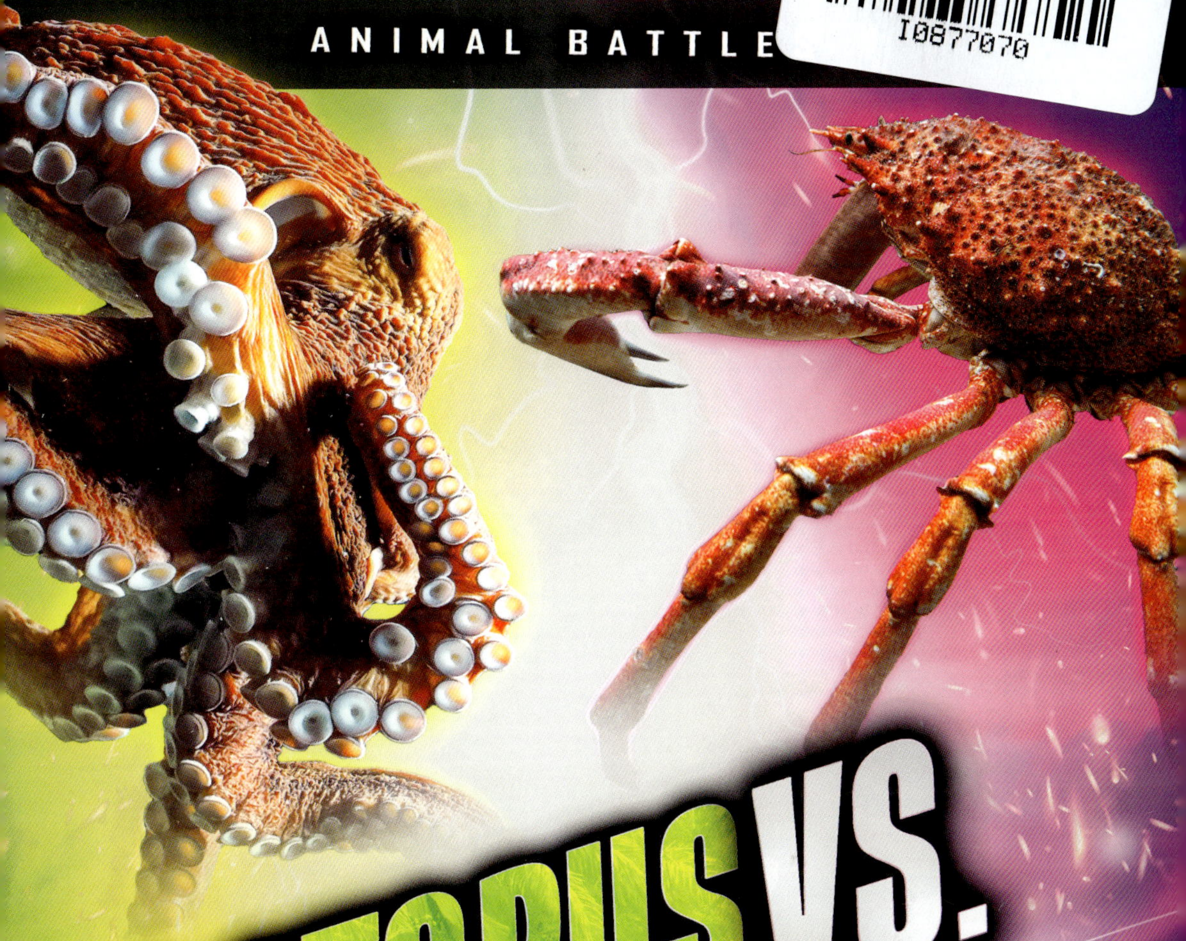

OCTOPUS VS. KING CRAB

BY NATHAN SOMMER

TORQUE™

TORQUE, AN IMPRINT OF BELLWETHER MEDIA BY FLUTTERBEE

Torque brims with excitement perfect for thrill-seekers of all kinds. Discover daring survival skills, explore uncharted worlds, and marvel at mighty engines and extreme sports. In *Torque* books, anything can happen. Are you ready?

This edition first published in 2027 by Bellwether Media, Inc.

Text copyright © 2027 by Bellwether Media, Inc. All rights reserved.
No part of this publication may be reproduced, stored in any retrieval system, or transmitted in any form or by any means, electronic, mechanical, photocopying, recording, or otherwise, without written permission of the publisher.

TORQUE and associated logos are trademarks and/or registered trademarks of Bellwether Media, Inc. Bellwether Media is a division of FlutterBee Education Group.

For information regarding permission, write to Bellwether Media, Inc., Attention: Permissions Department, 3500 American Blvd W, Suite 150, Bloomington, MN 55431.

Library of Congress Cataloging-in-Publication Data is available at www.loc.gov or upon request from the publisher.

ISBN: 9798898801151 (hardcover)
ISBN: 9798898802745 (paperback)
ISBN: 9798898802394 (ebook)

Editor: Suzane Nyguen Designer: Josh Brink

Printed in the United States of America, North Mankato, MN.

TABLE OF CONTENTS

THE COMPETITORS

The world's oceans are home to many **predators**. Octopuses are some of the smartest among them. They use large brains and many arms to outsmart and overpower **prey**.

Octopuses share some **habitats** with king crabs. These **crustaceans** use their shells and claws to defeat enemies. Who will win this underwater battle?

Octopuses are boneless **cephalopods**. They have soft, rounded bodies with eight sucker-covered arms. Their heads have large eyes and hard beaks.

There are about 300 **species** of octopuses. They are found in every ocean worldwide. Many live along the seafloor in shallow **tropical** waters. They often build dens in **coral reefs** or rock cracks.

GIANT PACIFIC OCTOPUS

A TIGHT SQUEEZE

Octopuses can squeeze their bodies through tiny openings. Some even fit through coin-sized holes!

GIANT PACIFIC OCTOPUS PROFILE

ARM SPAN

UP TO 14 FEET
(4.3 METERS)

HABITAT

OCEANS

WEIGHT

UP TO 110 POUNDS
(50 KILOGRAMS)

GIANT PACIFIC OCTOPUS RANGE

RED KING CRAB PROFILE

LEG SPAN

UP TO 5 FEET
(1.5 METERS)

WEIGHT

UP TO 24 POUNDS
(10.9 KILOGRAMS)

HABITATS

COLD OCEANS

MUDDY SEAFLOORS

RED KING CRAB RANGE

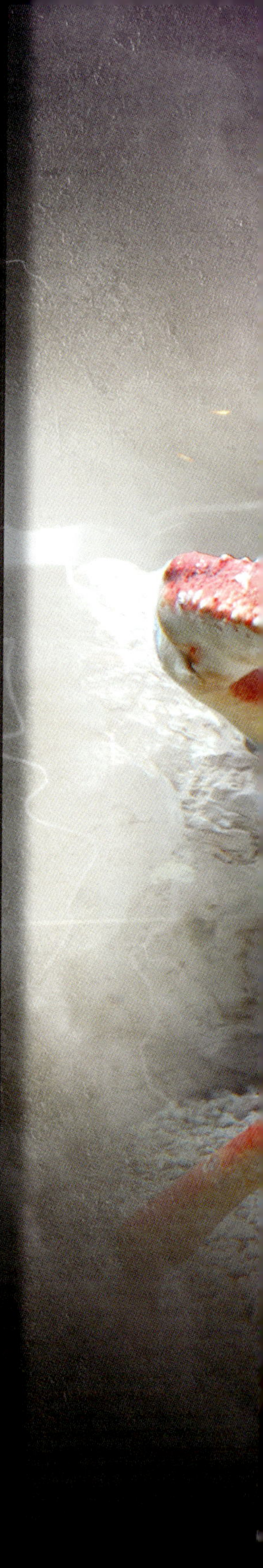

King crabs are some of the largest crabs. Their leg span can grow up to 5 feet (1.5 meters) wide. They have hard, spiky shells and long legs.

King crabs live along the seafloor of cold oceans. They prefer areas with sandy or muddy bottoms. Some are found up to 1,600 feet (488 meters) below the surface.

TRAVELING CRABS

Long legs help king crabs walk up to 8 miles (12.9 kilometers) per day.

SECRET WEAPONS

Octopuses are highly **intelligent**. Their large, donut-shaped brains give them good memories and help them use tools. They can solve problems to easily outsmart their prey.

LEG SPAN

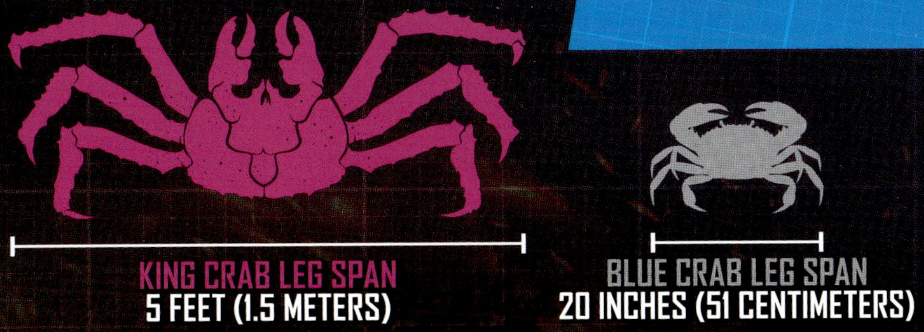

King crab bodies are covered in sharp spines. These make them painful for predators to touch and bite. Their shells keep their organs safe during enemy attacks.

SECRET WEAPONS

OCTOPUS

INTELLIGENCE

CAMOUFLAGE

FLEXIBLE ARMS

Special skin cells allow octopuses to **camouflage** instantly. They can quickly match the colors of their surroundings. This makes them almost impossible for other animals to spot.

SECRET WEAPONS

KING CRAB

SHARP SPINES

CHEMORECEPTORS

CLAWS

King crab legs have hairlike parts called **chemoreceptors**. These sense the **chemicals** given off by prey. The crabs can easily find their meals buried under sand.

ARM SPAN

Octopuses have strong, **flexible** arms. Each arm has its own mini-brain. This allows each arm to work separately. Suckers on the arms stick to prey. This makes it hard for prey to escape.

King crabs have two claws. Their larger claw crushes the shells of prey. Their smaller claw holds prey and cuts it into pieces.

ATTACK MOVES

WORKING WITH FISH

Octopuses sometimes hunt in groups with fish. The fish often find prey. The octopuses then choose what to hunt!

Octopuses often **ambush** prey from above. Some stick their arms into openings to feel for prey. They pull captured prey toward their sharp beaks. Beaks break shells and tear meat apart.

King crabs eat whatever they can catch. They travel the seafloor feeling and smelling for prey. Then they capture prey and crush it with their claws!

Octopuses shoot dark ink at enemies. Then they flush water through their bodies to escape quickly. Many slip through small cracks in rocks or change colors to hide.

Young king crabs form huge groups called pods. The group size scares off most predators. Adults have fewer enemies thanks to their shells. They also use their claws to fight.

THOUSANDS OF CRABS

The largest king crab pods can have up to 500,000 members.

READY, FIGHT!

A king crab passes beneath a camouflaged octopus. The octopus suddenly attacks from above. Its arm is cut by the crab's spine!

The crab fights back with its claws. The octopus pins it down using multiple arms. Its sharp beak then bites through the crab's shell to defeat it. The octopus's many arms overpowered the crab today!

GLOSSARY

ambush—to carry out a surprise attack

camouflage—to use colors and patterns to hide

cephalopods—sea creatures that have arms or tentacles connected directly to their heads

chemicals—materials that can cause a change in other materials

chemoreceptors—special cells that sense chemicals to help animals taste and smell their surroundings

coral reefs—structures made of coral that usually grow in shallow seawater

crustaceans—animals that have several pairs of legs and hard outer shells; lobsters and crabs are types of crustaceans.

flexible—able to bend easily

habitats—the homes or areas where animals prefer to live

intelligent—having the ability to learn or understand things

predators—animals that hunt other animals for food

prey—animals that are hunted by other animals for food

species—kinds of animals

tropical—having to do with a place that is hot and wet

TO LEARN MORE

AT THE LIBRARY

Clarke, Ginjer L. *Octopus!: Smartest in the Sea?* New York, N.Y.: Penguin Young Readers, 2024.

Gish, Melissa. *Crabs.* Mankato, Minn.: Creative Education and Creative Paperbacks, 2024.

Sommer, Nathan. *Octopus vs. Spiny Lobster.* Minneapolis, Minn.: Bellwether Media, 2025.

ON THE WEB

FACTSURFER

Factsurfer.com gives you a safe, fun way to find more information.

1. Go to www.factsurfer.com.
2. Enter "octopus vs. king crab" into the search box and click 🔍.
3. Select your book cover to see a list of related content

INDEX

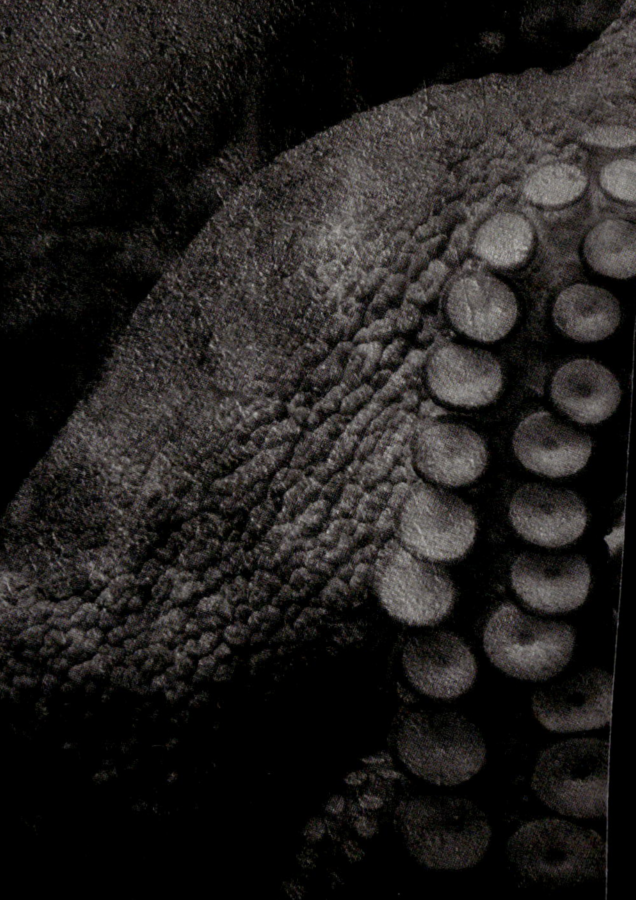

The images in this book are reproduced through the courtesy of: pr2is, front cover (octopus); Photosbypatrik, front cover (king crab); Azulblue, pp. 2 (octopus), 3 (octopus), 8-9, 20 (octopus), 21 (octopus), 22 (octopus), 23 (octopus), 24 (octopus); Larisa Blinova, pp. 2 (king crab), 3 (king crab), 20 (king crab), 21 (king crab), 22 (king crab), 23 (king crab), 24 (king crab); Diego Grandi, pp. 4, 12 (intelligence); scanout, pp. 5, 13 (chemoreceptors); Mikhail Blajenov, pp. 6-7; SergeUWPhoto, p. 10; Dmitri Portnov, p. 11; Irina Burakova, p. 11 (spines); A. Martin UWphoto, p. 12 (camouflage); EXTREME-PHOTOGRAPHER, p. 12 (flexible arms); Kevin Drew Davis, p. 12 (octopus); Gui_diaas, p. 13 (sharp spines); MingWei Chan, p. 13 (pair of claws); Jeff Mondragon/ Alamy Stock Photo, p. 13 (king crab); ArtWell, p. 14; kkolehma/ Getty Images, p. 15; Jeff Rotman/ Minden, p. 16; Heine Jensen, p. 17; Media Drum World/ Alamy Stock Photo, p. 18; Historic Collection/ Alamy Stock Photo, p. 19.